VIN DIESEL
XXXposeD

VIN DIESEL
XXXPOSED

Michael Robin and Todd Rone Owens

A ROUNDTABLE PRESS BOOK

POCKET BOOKS

New York   London   Toronto   Sydney   Singapore

An *Original* Publication of POCKET BOOKS

 POCKET BOOKS, a division of Simon & Schuster, Inc.
1230 Avenue of the Americas, New York, NY 10020

ISBN: 0-7434-7085-0

First Pocket Books trade paperback printing November 2002

10 9 8 7 6 5 4 3 2 1

POCKET and colophon are registered trademarks of Simon & Schuster, Inc.

For Roundtable Press, Inc.:
Directors: Julie Merberg and Marsha Melnick
Project Editor: Sara Newberry
Production Editor: John Glenn

Cover and Book Design: Charles Kreloff

Printed in the U.S.A.

For information regarding special discounts for bulk purchases, please contact Simon & Schuster Special Sales at 1-800-456-6798 or business@simonandschuster.com

PHOTO CREDITS: page 6: Tammie Arroyo/IPOL; pages 9, 15, 46, 51, 106, and 112: Ben Watts/Kramer & Kramer; page 11: MPTVA/HA-LFI; page 12: Alberto Lowe/Zuma Press; pages 16, 34, 41, 76 (bottom), 81, 82, 85, 87, 98, 100, and 110: Columbia Pictures/Zuma Press; page 19: Shark Pictures/Zuma Press; page 22: Jerzy Dabrowski/Zuma Press; pages 26, 31, 33, 36, and 42: Marsha Melnick; page 29: BEImages; page 38: Jeff Vespa/IPOL; pages 45, 52, 57, 60, 62, 64, 69, 70, 74, 76 (top), 79, 86, and 96: Photofest; page 72: Lisa O'Connor/Zuma Press; page 90: Lawrence Bender Productions/Zuma Press; page 94: Rena Durham/Zuma Press; page 97: Globe Photos; page 99: Big Pictures USA; page 102: George Campos/LFI; page 105: AP/Wide World Photos; page 108: Christina Radish/LFI

Chapter 1

Why Is the Big Man So Huge?

Vin Diesel is huge. Seemingly from nowhere, the man with the body of a giant and the voice to match has gone from a struggling actor to an Atlas carrying the future of American action film on his massive shoulders. He's king of the box office: his *xXx* knocked Mel Gibson from the top of the sales charts with a $44.5 million box-office jackpot in just its first three days of release. He's king of the newsstand: his Mount Rushmore–like head sneers, smiles, and scowls from the covers of magazines from *GQ* to *Savoy*. And he's king of the Internet, with fan pages blossoming every day, everywhere, and his name rapidly surpassing those of today's hottest film stars and models as the most searched on the web. But what accounts for the phenomenon that is Vin Diesel?

The future "king of the box office" in 2000

Timing Is Everything

Hollywood was starved for action heroes. The box office behemoths of yesteryear—Schwarzenegger and Stallone—are a touch past their prime. The martial artists who used to pick up the slack—Norris, Seagal, Van Damme—have faded from view. The few consistently persuasive movie tough guys—actors like Clint Eastwood and Sean Connery—aren't in their thirties . . . they were *born* in the '30s. Mel Gibson, Harrison Ford, and Russell Crowe chase Oscars in dramatic roles. Ben Affleck is more pretty than tough. Keanu Reeves would probably lose a fair fight with Carrie-Anne Moss. Rob Cohen, who directed Vin in *xXx* and *The Fast and the Furious*, tried to explain Vin's appeal to the *Toronto Sun*'s Bruce Kirkland: "In the past, action men have basically been killing machines who can make a joke. Vinny, on the other hand, has the courage to be overwhelmed and uncertain and sometimes to be almost nakedly needy."

What Makes Vin a Hero for the New Millennium?

Though Vin is continually compared to Stallone and Schwarzenegger, Bruce Willis is the action hero he most closely resembles (and it's more than scalp-deep). Like Willis, Vin has a certain postmodern sensibility; he's in on the joke. His action heroes treat every situation they're placed in with appropriate seriousness, yet Vin also seems liable at any second to look right into the camera, smirk, and ask, "Did you guys get a load of that one?"

As *Salon* put it, "In a way, he's the perfect twenty-first-century hero: a bad guy who's really a good guy, who isn't necessarily Wittgenstein but is certainly smarter than he looks."

Vin in his downtown-NYC stomping ground, 2002

So what is it exactly that guides Vin in his choice of these kinds of characters? What is the "new thing" that he brings to the table? Vin told Zap2it.com, "My characters start as underdogs . . . and allow the audience to become heroic with the character." Or as *xXx* director Rob Cohen put it, "In the case of Vinny, he's a true antihero. He's an anti-establishment, anti-authoritarian badass." Okay, but is that so novel? Haven't we seen that before in heroes ranging from Clint Eastwood's Dirty Harry to Wesley Snipes's Blade? No, because these classic anti-heroes were essentially idealists, resisting chaos, fighting to maintain some kind of order in a world that had lost its balance. But for Vin's Xander, order and balance themselves are the enemy. Chaos isn't bad, it's fun. As Xander himself says, "If you send someone to save the world, make sure they like it the way it is."

One Race . . . What Race?

With his olive skin, full lips, and indeterminate nose, no one (except his mother) has any idea what ethnicity Vin Diesel actually is, and he likes it that way. Though rumored to be of African and Italian heritage, Vin refuses to get specific. He's named his production company One Race and describes himself only as "multicultural." He told *Time* magazine, "I support the idea of being multicultural primarily for all the invisible kids, the ones who don't fit into one ethnic category and then find themselves lost in some limbo."

A One Race staff member has said that Vin is Irish, Italian, German, Dominican, Mexican, and a lot of other things. In 1999, at a party at New York City's Joe's Pub, he was seen sporting a large Star of David tattoo. When asked if he was Jewish, he replied, "For now."

"I like that I'm multicultural, I embrace my racial ambiguity," he says. "I love to empower people. I love sending the message you can create your dream, you can do whatever you want to do." Ben Younger, Vin's director in *Boiler Room*, has proposed that people make Vin into whatever they want him to be, and that is one of the primary reasons for his popularity. As Vin told the paper *UniverCity* when they asked what he considered himself ethnically, "If you just want a white, black, Latin answer . . . it's definitely not that simple . . . I will probably be one of a few actors that defies all barriers—at least, I hope I do. So far I have played all types of roles and ethnicities. Whereas that ambiguity might have been a curse to me earlier in my life, it's actually a blessing now."

In an interview with the Associated Press, Vin employed an interesting political metaphor to try to explain his philosophy: "I like to go into roles without being, y'know, Monica Lewinsky. Imagine Monica Lewinsky or President Clinton trying to do a film. I'm just saying that I do a better job if I'm only accepted as the role that I'm playing."

Vin, sporting a Star of David tattoo, in a scene from *Knockaround Guys*, 2002

What People Are Saying About Vin's Voice

"A gravelly baritone."
—Mark Salisbury, *Premiere*

"A sultry basso profundo."
—Gil Robertson, *Savoy*

"A laughing street rumble with a slightly acrid, burned-onion edge."
—David Denby, *The New Yorker*

"A computer-generated version of James Earl Jones."
—Jamie Allen, *CNN Interactive*

"Both raspily deep and almost femininely delicate." —Bob Strauss, Associated Press

"Guttural." —*AskMen*

"The voice of the devil." —Rob Cohen

"Sounds like he chews glass and swallows." —*Rolling Stone*

"A voice that would even irritate Barry White." —*Niewe Revu*

"So deep only Bea Arthur can imitate it." —Jess Cagle, *Time*

"So low, it's a wonder it doesn't set off car alarms." —Benjamin Svetkey, *Entertainment Weekly*

At the premiere of the film *Tigerland*, 2000

That Voice

Let's face it, this book probably wouldn't be in your hands if Vin Diesel sounded like Rosie Perez. Nine years as a bouncer taught him how to let words land, how to face down an angry mob that outnumbered him twenty to one, and how to let them know in no uncertain terms, "You are not getting in tonight." A barrel chest that displaces more air than a locomotive powers the imperious rasp.

The Brain

"He's smart," Asia Argento, his *xXx* love interest, unambiguously asserted to *People*, dashing the hopes of guys everywhere who'd hoped there was at least one category in which they had Vin Diesel beat. During filming, Argento recalled, Vin "explained the scene and what my character was thinking. There was a director quality there." In an interview with IGN.com, Argento admitted to being surprised by more than his intelligence. "He's a very down-to-earth person, very giving. I have never worked with an actor who is so not self-centered and so ready to help."

There is no question that having Vin Diesel on the set keeps directors on their toes. Listen to his commentary on the *Pitch Black* DVD: Vin constantly assesses shots, lenses, lighting, and performances, voicing his opinions with the same authority that he brings to his screen dialogue. Any director not at the top of his game would be blown away. On the other hand, like-minded directors such as *xXx*'s Rob Cohen and *Pitch Black*'s David Twohy say that Vin's demanding intelligence elevates their own performances and results in better films.

Vin Diesel knows how to use his head. In fact, Vin spreading axle grease all over it is one of the most arresting images in *Pitch Black*. Is he camouflaging it from alien eyes? Masking it from their sonar? No . . . he's shaving it! Vin has, in one stroke, raised the bar for movie tough guys (would Rambo trim his stubble with axle grease and a metal shard?) and overshadowed a multimillion dollar special effects budget with nothing more than his personal grooming habits.

What People Are Saying About Vin's Head

"Shiny pate."—*People*

"Bulging."—*AskMen*

"Aerodynamically correct."—*Salon*

"Bedpan headed."—Lisa Schwarzbaum, *Entertainment Weekly*

"I'm actually getting kind of thin in some areas."—Vin, in *People*

New York City, 2002

The Brawn

Ah, the Kryptonics. That's Vin's nickname (taken from a brand of skateboard wheel) for those tree-trunk biceps he so often bares on screen. Vin's finely sculpted 225-pound frame has helped him muscle past the other contenders for the action movie throne, but he's careful to keep his shirt on long enough to avoid the *Conan the Barbarian* trap. He wants the freedom enjoyed by stars like Mel Gibson, whom audiences accept in both dramatic and action roles. Sorry, fans, that means the Kryptonics will stay in their holsters at least part of the time.

Though Vin's muscles were integral in cementing his superstardom, they weren't always an asset. Vin had lobbied for the role of the sassy, cussing drag queen in the 1999 drama *Flawless*, opposite Robert De Niro. Vin felt he was uniquely suited for the part due to his familiarity with the

Where Art Thou, Vin?

"As an actor, I'm a canvas," Diesel told *USA Today*. "That's the reality for me. I wouldn't be able to create new ones for each role." So the following is a list of some of the "paint" that has covered the Diesel canvas.

"xXx" on the back of his neck

Charging bull coming out of clouds and flames; tribal band

Star with eye in center; the word *chaos*; another bull; three stars; an eagle; the word *disorder*

The name Melkor (Vin's favorite Dungeons & Dragons character) on his stomach; flaming chaos symbol around his belly button; star around his nipple

Crossed guns on the small of his back

Vin in *xXx*: he definitely ain't your daddy's James Bond

transvestites of Manhattan's West Village and the club world. But director Joel Schumacher turned Diesel down. As Vin told *Time* magazine, "A transvestite spends her life trying to look as feminine as possible, and . . . I have obviously spent my life celebrating my masculinity"—along with the rest of the world. It just shows that things work out for the best; would we really have wanted to see Vin wearing a dress, weeping at De Niro's feet, mascara running down his damp cheeks? Let's say it together: "Thank you, Mr. Schumacher!"

Not that we haven't enjoyed seeing Vin shed a tear or two on screen. Part of his characters' appeal is that beneath their hard surfaces lie tender souls. Xander Cage weeps when Yorgi, *xXx*'s anarchistic arch-villain, gasses a roomful of scientists. The glow-in-the-dark eyes of Richard Riddick (*Pitch Black*) fill with tears when a comrade dies in his arms. Vin Diesel is one of the few action heroes tough enough to cry.

The Tattoos

Sorry, fans, but off-camera Vin is tattoo-free. That's right, Xander Cage's blazing body art was one of *xXx*'s most special effects. And a pretty pricey one at that: The elaborate decals that were used to apply his colorful tattoos reportedly cost forty thousand dollars. Although they took two hours to put on, they saved time in the long run; instead of requiring a daily touch-up like most hand-drawn movie tattoos, they lasted two to three days. "Most of the tattoos you see in the movies are drawn on daily at the studio with a pen and India ink or even a Sharpie," explained tattoo parlor owner Dusty Geisman in the *Los Angeles Daily News*.

Like everything in *xXx*, the body art was carefully thought out. Rob Cohen wanted decoration that would both emphasize Xander Cage's chaotic spirit and look sexy even to fans who hated tattoos.

The Attitude

After *The Fast and the Furious* (2001) assured Vin Diesel's position as the newest and brightest star in the Hollywood firmament, there came a certain amount of the requisite backlash. Many agents, displaying classic sour grapes, whined that Vin's rise was pure dumb luck, the result of him being in the right place at the right time. The implication was that Vin did nothing to earn his success. Of course, nothing could be further from the truth. Vin's success is largely the result of an attitude he cultivated for years, a determination and self-confidence he had to gird himself with in order to survive the spirit-crushing pressures of the film industry. The quotes on the following page, all Vin's, can be construed as representing the philosophy he adopted in order to conquer Hollywood.

❝ I may not be that smart. I may not be that good-looking. But cool? Yes. Very cool. ❞

—Vin, *Premiere*

At the premiere of *xXx*, 2002

What Vin Says
About His Attitude

"I ignored the relevance of understanding the industry. I was just this guy in New York thinking of how to get that moment alive and how to be truthful. I spent twenty years trying to be truthful—and unemployed."

—Action Adventure

"It's all about determination and persistence—which is why you should be passionate about what you're doing. Because it is really tough after you've written your script. It's you versus the world. So get your team together, and get your confidence together."

—Writers Guild forum, 1997

"People keep asking if I've changed since becoming a celebrity. But I haven't changed because I've always thought I was a celebrity. It was the rest of the world that hadn't figured it out."

—Entertainment Weekly

"It all came down to me having to believe in myself and forgetting about what the rest of the world thought.'"

—Savoy

"You have to feel somewhat cool about yourself if you're going to be that extroverted and be that outgoing. If you really believe that you have something to contribute, and in this circumstance a certain art medium, then you really have to believe it and you should dedicate your life to it."

—Access Hollywood on MSN

"I'm trying to make the most of the little I have."

—Attributed to Vin by friend Adrian Brody in *Rolling Stone*

The Man of Mystery

Vin Diesel is larger than life and is fast developing a mythology to match. He almost seems to dare the public to keep up with him as rumors proliferate about his background, his love life, and his next film. He seems to share a philosophy with Dominic Toretto, the street-racing character he played in last year's smash hit *The Fast and the Furious*: no rearview mirror, no speedometer, no looking back. Especially no looking back. Vin Diesel is notoriously quiet about his past, politely but firmly deflecting questions that feel too personal. Many stars evade questions about their dating habits, but Vin even brushes aside questions about what he eats. Of course this has only fed the fans' frenzy. Rumors flood in to fill the void. But beneath the carefully managed movie star exterior lies a story as compelling as anything on the screen. It's time to set the record straight. Let's look in the rearview mirror.

Chapter 2

Growing Up Vin, I Mean Mark

Vin Diesel was born Mark Vincent on July 18, 1967, along with his fraternal twin brother, Paul, in the middle of the infamous and *Sgt. Pepper's* dominated Summer of Love. Even in utero, Vin was competing for attention. The boys' mother, Delora, was an astrologer, and although she has always claimed to be too close to her son to be able to read his future objectively, young Vin would soon study her books and learn that he's a Cancer, with Scorpio rising and a Sagittarius moon. All you astrology skeptics, you may want to reconsider: Scorpio rising is associated with a strong physique and tremendous physical stamina, as well as tremendous tenacity. And having a moon in Sagittarius suggests that you crave adventure.

At the BAFTA/LA Britannia Awards, 2000

Vin's Stars

Having grown up under the influence of the stars with an astrologer mother, one wonders what she might have forecast for her star-in-the-making son.

BIRTHDAY: July 18, 1967
SIGN: Cancer   SYMBOL: The Crab
COLOR: Silver   STARSTONE: Pearl

The Cancerian Character

There are a number of traits associated with Vin's sun sign, Cancer. Some of the more notable characteristics which might loosely apply to Vin include:

• A HOME-LOVING NATURE. Cancer men appreciate having a comfortable "nest" they can withdraw or escape to when life's stresses overwhelm them. They consider the home more of a cozy den—a place that belongs to the family—than a possession designed to impress others. Vin does share his current home with his sister. . .

• THICK SKIN. This outer toughness often hides a sensitive heart. It is also associated with tremendous tenacity.

• A VIVID IMAGINATION. Interestingly enough, Cancerians are appreciative of drama. They are also prone to fantasy, which goes a long way towards explaining the Dungeons and Dragons fixation.

• A SHARP EAR. Cancerians can be good mimics, making them especially suited for acting.

• PROTECTIVE INSTINCTS. Cancerians are loyal to family and friends, and see themselves as protectors.

• IMPRESSIONABLE PERSONALITY. Cancerians can be easily influenced by those they love. Also, their ambition may lead them to switch loyalties (or to adopt the positions of others) if doing so advances their own personal cause.

And, of course, there's lots of Cancerian stuff that doesn't apply at all to Vin (or at least to the Vin that we know).

Is Vin His Birth Date?

Some interesting (and slightly more specific) tidbits emerged from a chart based on Vin's birthday (as opposed to his sun sign). According to astrology.com, Vin has "a great affinity for music, because it evokes and communicates feelings that may be difficult or impossible to put into words." Oddly enough, this same profile predicts that Vin is "not especially confident about speaking in public." Good thing he built up his confidence.

Vin's Love Signs

Cancer's most compatible signs are Scorpio, Pisces, Taurus, and Virgo.

Potential mates should keep the following in mind: Cancerians' homey nature means they like to keep a low profile. A cozy dinner at home is much more appealing than a night on the town (unless it involves dancing, of course). Cancerians can also be very emotional and sentimental. And they hate confrontation.

Everybody has a Mars and a Venus, and these planets rule the love, lust, and romance in our lives. Mars influences how we initiate relationships, and Venus, the planet of love, determines what makes us feel special and adored.

• VIN'S MARS IS IN LIBRA. This means that he's smart, charming, and attractive. And once again, he hates confrontation (very interesting considering those bouncing days . . .). But Libra's desire to please also makes for romance.

• VIN'S VENUS IS IN VIRGO. Echoing Asia Argento's assessment, those with a Venus in Virgo are typically down-to-earth. On the relationship front, this translates to a fuss-free partner. Vin should attract lovers who appreciate his simple nesting instinct and aren't looking for flash (which they'll get anyhow).

The Westbeth housing complex, Vin's childhood home and the current home of his parents

As for Vin's biological father, Vin has never met the man and claims that he has no desire to meet him. He knows that he's alive, and that's all. The man that Vin calls "Dad" is his stepfather, Irving Vincent, a theater director and teacher whom Vin idolizes to this day. Young Vin would watch Irving come home still in costume after an evening's performance and perhaps dream of following in his father's footsteps.

Vin, Paul, and their younger sister Samantha grew up in the Westbeth Artists Housing complex in New York City's Greenwich Village. (They also have a much younger brother who is currently in his teens.) Built in the late 1960s to provide affordable housing for artists and their families, the complex is a cluster of plain-looking high-rise buildings near the Hudson River. Though located on the bustling, crowded island of Manhattan, Greenwich Village was once an independent municipality and has retained a distinctive character to this day. The Village's annexation by New York

City did nothing to unravel the mystery of its cantilevered streets, which run at angles to the rest of Manhattan's simplistic grid, resulting in a confusing snarl where West 4th Street runs both north and south of West 10th Street depending on where you are, and taxi drivers have been confusing Greenwich Street with Greenwich Avenue since time immemorial. The cobblestone cross streets are a little quieter, the buildings are a little shorter; Greenwich Village is, in short, a neighborhood like no other in New York, one that has long attracted writers, artists, oddballs, and nonconformists of every stripe. It was the center of the Beat movement in the 1950s, the gay pride movement in the '60s, and antiwar activism in the '70s. The Westbeth apartments, located at the far end of the Village's tangle, tower over this unruly kingdom. The nearby meatpacking district is a place where commerce both illicit and legitimate rages long into the night, where butchers, hustlers, students, tourists, and drag queens share the sidewalks until dawn. It's a neighborhood of colorful characters. In the Village, outrageousness was the norm, and Vin Diesel was right at home.

Early on, the Vincents knew young Vin had the show business bug. When he was three years old, his mother took him to see the Ringling Bros. and Barnum & Bailey circus. In the middle of the show, with lions, horses, and elephants racing and roaring around the rings, young Vin climbed from his seat and tried to join them! Delora snatched him to safety and asked what he was doing. "Mommy, I'm ready to do my show now," came Vin's reply. Even at a tender age, he knew where he belonged.

Poor but Happy

Vin describes his childhood as poor but happy. The family couldn't afford tickets to Yankees or Knicks games, but Vin played a lot of basketball in the public parks. He remembers his father pulling him and his brother around on a cheap red sled in the snow in Washington Square Park. In summer, his mother would take him wading in the park's huge central fountain. Vin became the ringleader of a group of kids that tore around the neighborhood on their banana-seat bikes looking for trouble. He'd duck into the local restaurants and wash a few dishes in return for french fries. The fries must have seemed like a special treat since greasy foodstuffs were rare at home. In an era when most moms considered it a noble dietary sacrifice to switch from white sugar to brown, Delora was a health-conscious parent who made her children's toast and sandwiches with multigrain bread, and banned soft drinks from the apartment. If Vin was a wild child, it wasn't because of sugar overload. Even that childhood staple, frosted breakfast cereal in milk, sugar-thickened to the consistency of cement, was forbidden. Vin would sleep over at friends' houses just to get his early morning Sugar Smacks fix.

Vin always recalls his childhood with obvious joy. The family had money only for necessities (no wonder he now spends so much time glued to his beloved video games!) but Vin and his crew of mischief makers made their own fun. In a neighborhood spilling over with entertainers, it must have seemed the normal thing to do. Vin remembers that most of the kids he hung out with were multi-racial; even in this regard he fit right in. With all of New York City as his stage, each day must have brought with it the promise of new adventures.

There were two luxuries for which the Vincents shared an appreciation, and those were theater and film. Whenever Irving took Vin to the local cinema or a nearby Off-Broadway showcase, they always spent hours afterward talking about what they'd seen. These conversations helped lay the groundwork for both Vin's future career and a lifelong parent-child bond. "My father didn't take us to baseball games or basketball games," Vin told *MadBlast.com*. "We didn't have the money to do all that so our father and son experience was he'd take us to movies and at the end of the movie we'd go get a $1.50 plate of chicken lo mein on 42nd Street and rap about the movie. . . . We'd be talking about *My Fair Lady* or *Guys and Dolls* on one level and then a Sidney Poitier–directed movie like *Uptown Saturday Night.* Just everything." At some point Vin began to imagine himself up there on the screen. "I can do that," he thought. He was right, but it wasn't quite musical theater that Vin was destined for.

Vin like TV.

The First Gig

Little did young Mark Vincent suspect that his first big break was right around the corner—literally! Vin's most eye-opening visit to the theater came when he was seven years old. He and a band of eight pint-sized troublemakers that included his brother, Paul, were pedaling around the neighborhood when somebody noticed a theater's unguarded open door. Like junior versions of *Mad Max*'s motorcycle miscreants, Vin and company ditched their three-speeds and swarmed into the theater like locusts.

Crystal Field, the artistic director of Theater for the New City, was alone inside when Vin and his merry band of marauders began running amok. She recalls the nerve-racking moment: "Our doors are always open, so anybody can just walk in. They don't unless they're interested in the theater. . . or they're a thief."

Despite the threatening situation, Field, a self-described pacifist, decided to confront the intruders. "I had to dilute violence," she recalls. "When the bear comes after you, you throw something or scream at it." She chose the latter, walking onto the stage and ordering Vin, Paul, and their accomplices to show themselves. They reluctantly obeyed, Vin creeping down from the mezzanine. Drawing upon her years of experience making theater with at-risk youth in disadvantaged neighborhoods, Field looked over the clean,

❝ I didn't know Vin Diesel was Mark Vincent! He had hair when I knew him! ❞

—Crystal Field

Theater for the New City, at its new East Village location

well-dressed Vin and made this assessment: "He was a rebel without a cause." Anticipating a scolding, Vin and his cohorts received something entirely different . . . scripts!

Field happened to be in the process of casting a play called *The Dinosaur Door* by Barbara Garson. Why not join the theater instead of trashing it? "It's just as exciting," she promised Vin, "and you'll have a great time." Vin Diesel had landed his first acting job! For $20 a week (a mere six zeroes shy of his payday for the *xXx* sequel), he and Paul went to the theater every day after school at four o'clock and learned their lines. "We had to keep them creatively occupied during rehearsal," Field remembers, "otherwise they became destructive." Volunteers stood by with crayons and paper for Vin when he came off stage, the childhood equivalent of his laptop.

The production was a smashing success. Vin played a third grader who gets lost in New York's Museum of Natural History and wanders through a door that leads to the land of the dinosaurs. There were songs about everything from archaeology to food additives. The show ran for ten weeks and won Off-Broadway's prestigious Obie Award. Let's all hope Vin will someday appear in the revival.

These days Vin is considering hosting an emerging playwrights' festival at Theater for the New City, demonstrating how connected he is with his roots. "I wish him great luck," says Field, "I'm so pleased he became famous." She remembers loving Vin's performance in *Saving Private Ryan*, only, "I didn't know Vin Diesel was Mark Vincent! He had hair when I knew him!"

Was Vin's second stage appearance a fluke? (His first stage role was two years earlier, when he played a horse in *Cinderella*.) Crystal Field doesn't think so: "Why break into a theater? Something deep inside him impelled him to come through that door."

Vin himself might agree. Life was getting tougher as he was getting older. For the first time, the lack of multicultural role models in popular culture began to affect him. He was starting to feel different. And for a boy his age, different wasn't necessarily a good thing. Playing a character was a way for Vin Diesel to give himself an identity. He has described his childhood acting roles as "therapeutic."

Irving continued to nurture Vin's interest in the theater, involving him in Off-Off-Broadway productions throughout his childhood. "Triple-off, off Broadway was a luxury," he told *Access* magazine. Though theater provided his introduction to acting, Vin stated that he prefers filmmaking to theater due to the immortal nature of film. In addition, he explained, "I like the capability of perfecting it and enhancing the story, reworking a story. . . . Theater is a one-shot deal. You get on stage and it begins and that's the experience—and that's cool." Vin has also claimed that he doesn't need the immediate gratification, the instant audience response that so many actors relish about working on stage.

School Days

At home, he curled up with classic books as well as comic books. Out in the streets, though, his stunts got more extreme. When he wasn't reciting imaginary lines on the subway, Vin was climbing between moving cars and shimmying up to their roofs. He and his friends would rollerblade around town, grabbing on to buses and taxis for treacherous high-speed joyrides. It all foreshadowed *xXx*; New York was continuously providing training to the boy that would some day serve the man.

In 1970s, Irving and Delora enrolled Vin and his brother, Paul, in Manhattan's Anglo-American International School, whose famous alumni include New York mayor Fiorello LaGuardia, Broadway director Hal Prince, and three members of the band The Strokes. The school's global

Vin riding his tray in *xXx*. Do not try this in your cafeteria.

focus drew students from all over the world; many of the fifty-six students in Vin's grade were from overseas. Once again Vin was safely ensconced in a place where everyone was a little "different." Maybe that sense of security engendered at school motivates his recent declarations that if he hadn't gone into acting, he'd be a school principal.

A maintenance man still employed there recalls that one of the Vincent boys was a great dancer. We can probably guess which one. In 1984, Vin made his film debut in an instructional break-dancing video entitled *Breakin' in the U.S.A.* According to the Southern Indiana Education Center Video Catalog, the fifty-minute tape offers "break dancing taught by the pros. . . . Gives detailed instructions on warming up, dressing right, and dance techniques. Learn the Electric Boogie, Moonwalk, Spin Glide, the Rope, the Wall, the Robot, and more." During high school, Vin would strut his stuff at Studio 54 and Danceteria. Vin's plea to Asia Argento in *xXx*, "I'm a really good dancer!" was apparently no idle boast. Too bad he didn't prove it with the Electric Boogaloo.

A Voice Is Born

Adolescence brought the usual big changes, although in Vin's case some were unusually big. At thirteen, his voice got deeper. And deeper. And deeper. Kids teased him; their mothers flirted. Vin was puzzled by the reactions to his new voice, and embarrassed by comparisons with Barry White. The Adolescent Vin could never suspect that in twenty years there would be an entire generation of mothers and (more importantly) daughters who would be swooning at the rumble of that distinctly deep voice.

The Tunnel, where Vin served as bouncer and doorman

Where'd the Girls Go?

Vin claims that he was never very popular with girls his age. He wasn't the sort of pretty boy that girls chased after. His looks were not what could be considered your classical chiseled features à la Leonardo DiCaprio or Brad Pitt. His distinctive nose certainly becomes more lovable when attached to a sculpted body and a $20 million paycheck. So, having not yet grown into his unique looks, Vin often found himself doing the running, trying to catch girls before they disappeared into the subway. Most of those girls are probably kicking themselves furiously today.

The brazen kid who had swaggered through childhood with unshakeable self-assurance was now a teenager looking for ways to build confidence. One way was by building muscle; at fifteen, Vin started working out, first at Greenwich House, then Carmine's, then at Gleason's gym. His fitness regimen was an obsession that would serve him well. After his 1985 graduation from Anglo-American, Vin's size helped win him a job as a bouncer at some of Manhattan's hottest nightclubs, including Tunnel and Mars, where the up-and-coming Moby spun his music. It was during this time that he found another way of building his confidence. Mark Vincent took the name that he bears to this day: Vin Diesel.

Although he changed his name to further his career as a bouncer, Vin Diesel was following in the footsteps of some of Hollywood's sexiest tough guys. Since the early days of film, the names that send hearts aflutter have very often been different from the ones their owners were born with. Rock Hudson, for example, came into the world as Roy Scherer, Jr. Cary Grant was formerly known as Archibald Leach. Woody Allen was born Allen Konigsberg. Even one of Vin's cinematic idols, Kirk Douglas, is not what he seems: Kirk Douglas started life as Issur Danielovitch. *Mark Vincent*'s got nothing on *Issur*.

Chapter 3

Bouncing His Way Up

Always be nice to your doorman, 'cause you never know if he may become one of the biggest stars in the world! Not since Mr. T has an ex-bouncer become so famous, and Mr. T didn't even have the guts to shave his whole head.

Ricky Mercado, owner of the popular New York nightspots Club Speeed and Opaline, was Vin's general manager at Tunnel. He recalls the balance of looks, presence, and social skills that made Vin the perfect match for a security staff that had to manage a celebrity-laden crowd. Vin was "a stand-up guy" who "took the time to get to know people," and became a well-known figure at the club. When there was trouble, Vin, although he was "nonfearing of any confrontation," would always try to "talk it out first."

Vin, showing a little of the attitude that made him a successful NYC bouncer

Vin came into the club, even on his nights off, to dance. "People were impressed," remembers Mercado. Vin had no inhibitions about dancing alone and drew a lot of attention from the ladies. A rumor spread that John Travolta had seen Vin dance at Tunnel and flew him out to Los Angeles for a private lesson. Laughs Mercado, "I know Travolta came in. I know that they spoke." Whether the rest is true or the stuff of urban legend is unknown. Either way, it's clear that even in Tunnel's celebrity-laden environment, Vin fit right in.

Upon becoming stars, many actors credit their old acting instructors or talk about the importance of the Method or Shakespeare in the Park. The Method may help prepare one to tackle Eugene O'Neill, but Eugene didn't write action films. Vin had to develop his own "method." If his screen characters keep a cool head under pressure, it's because the man who portrays them learned to do the same. Vin's real-life exploits may not quite equal those of, say, Xander Cage, but his bouncer years included plenty of hair-raising (so to speak) episodes. Vin has said that he witnessed shootings and stabbings, and singlehandedly fought groups of angry guys.

Vin considered it a good night if he only got into one fight. Some bosses would slip him an extra $25 to go into the street and confront scalpers who had sold club or party invitations to the riffraff. This was tough stuff; a fellow bouncer actually had his throat slit in the line of duty. Vin often refers to the risks he took on the job as "stupid" and "asinine." But he needed the money to support his plan to go to college and his acting ambitions. Besides, there were other perks of life inside the velvet rope. For the first time, women wanted to talk to Vin. If they wanted to get into the club, well, he was the man in charge. All that working out probably didn't hurt either; Vin kept himself in shape by boxing at the gym. Time spent watching the door at New York's trendiest spots also honed his fashion sense. Vin bought stylish clothes, provided he could return them if money was tight at the end of the month. And it's no easy task for a bouncer to keep his clothes stain- and

"See, if I push down like this, it makes my triceps look even bigger!"

blood-free. He remained a bouncer for nine years, but Vin always kept his sights on bigger things, studying acting and auditioning during the day and planning for his big break.

The job certainly built character. Vin learned to be diplomatic, to deal tactfully with club goers of every description, to defuse confrontations, and to take care of himself if things got rough. He must have found it ironic when in *Boiler Room* (2000) his character was actually thrown out of a bar by a bouncer, yet if you look carefully at the scene you'll notice that the actor playing the bouncer wisely steers clear of Vin.

But there was a downside to living the hard life. When Vin went on auditions, he could never quite turn off his bouncer persona.

"I had to be as amiable as possible," he told the Associated Press. "But I still had this edge, this threatening physical presence. So you can come into a room and say, 'Hi, my name is Vin Diesel.' But you have the 'If you don't like me, I'll punch you in the face,' kind of feel, which is not what you really want to do when you're going on auditions."

Desperate Years

After finishing high school, Diesel enrolled in New York's prestigious Hunter College as a theater major. After careful consultation with his father, whose judgment he continued to value, and based on the advice of

The 6-train subway stop for Hunter College

friends in the business, he switched to an English major. The change would allow Vin to focus more on writing, a skill he knew might someday prove useful. If the film community didn't provide him with the roles he sought, he just might have to write them for himself.

Vin's patience ran out before he had earned his degree from Hunter. Frustrated with the New York film scene, he packed his bags and set out for Los Angeles. Never mind that he was ten thousand dollars in debt, or that he had no solid prospects in L.A. Or that he hadn't quite finished college.

The Wrong Kind of Success

Vin took a job selling lightbulbs as a telemarketer (something a young and undiscovered Jerry Seinfeld did as well), certain that it was only a matter of time before his hard work and perseverance would pay off. No such luck. Los Angeles didn't know what to make of Vin Diesel either. His indeterminate ethnicity puzzled casting directors. What was he, exactly? Unable to pigeonhole the big New Yorker, they turned him away.

Soon Vin found himself putting in enormous amounts of time at his telemarketing job just to work off his debts. The long hours on the phone paid off; Vin made good money and earned recognition for his success as a salesman. Perhaps the forceful voice and personality that served him so well at the nightclub door terrified the people at the other end of the line into giving up their cash. The money added up, but the hours took a toll: Vin was doing well, but not in his chosen profession. The Los Angeles adventure had gone terribly awry. It was time to go home.

Making Lemonade

Vin returned to New York in his words, "with my tail between my legs." It was a low point that would have driven many to let go of their dreams. Not our hero. While again working as a bouncer, he redoubled his writing efforts, determined to write for himself the role that Hollywood wouldn't provide. Even the telemarketing misadventure had provided him with tools that he could use to his advantage. In the film business, there are few talents more important than the ability to talk people out of their money.

This period of Vin's life, his early twenties, wasn't all about struggle and hardship. Remember, he had learned early in life how to get by with very little. After a guy's shared a uterus for nine months, a night on a friend's sofa is no big deal. A lack of resources never came between Vin and a good time. In a pinch, he and his buddies could always schmooze a free meal out of friendly (and more than likely female) fast food counterfolk. They would even go on road trips with only a few dollars in their pockets. Vin remembers once making his way across half the continent to Cancun, Mexico, on little more than his smooth tongue and irresistible charm.

In the wake of Vin's discouraging California trip, his mother gave him a book called *Feature Films at Used Car Prices* by Rick Schmidt. It was just the push he needed. Vin drew on everything he'd been through: the writing talent he'd developed in college; the salesmanship he'd perfected while telemarketing; the people skills he'd picked up at the clubs; the hard-won experience earned during years of being turned away by an industry with no place for multicultural performers. The result was *Multi-Facial.* Vin was finally taking his destiny into his own hands.

Vin calls on his telemarketing past for *Boiler Room*.

Chapter 4

Making His Own Breaks

"When you write independent film, not only do you think about all of your resources, but you've got to pick something that you know," said Vin at a 1997 panel discussion presented by the Writers Guild Foundation. One of the things Vin knew best was the host of challenges faced by multicultural actors, so in 1994 he wrote, produced, directed, and starred in a short film on that very subject. He raised money, called in favors, did whatever it took to make his project happen. His brother, Paul, lent a hand as sound editor. "If you do a film that you know," said Vin during the panel discussion, "you'll do it better than somebody with $60 million." Shot for just three thousand dollars, *Multi-Facial* proved his point.

Pensive in NYC, 2002

Multi-Facial

Ruth Otero, a solo performer whom *Variety* named one of 2002's "Ten Comics to Watch," remembers the audition that won her a role in *Multi-Facial*. "Vin knew just the right way to compliment a performer," she says. She describes a classic "guerilla filmmaking" shoot during which cast and crew raced around New York City trying to get shots in before sunset.

Not once during the frantic schedule did Vin's self-assurance slip. Though success was still years away, he already carried himself like a star. "He was so smooth," Otero recalls, "he seemed like a Hollywood player." In fact, Vin already had an entourage of sorts! "He'd surrounded himself with people who believed in him. He seemed to have a mission and a lot of support behind him." Vin's belief in himself was contagious. Predicted one cast member: "He's gonna be huge!"

A rare moment of self-revelation came when Vin heard "You Gotta Be," Des'ree's 1994 chart-topping ode to positive thinking, on Otero's answering machine. "I've got that song on my machine, too," he said. "It's my mantra."

He'd need a good mantra. Negative feedback almost kept *Multi-Facial* from ever making it to the screen. The comments of people who had trouble seeing past Vin's identity as a bouncer and down-and-out actor led him to abandon the film before its final edit. Fortunately, his father, Irving, intervened.

❝ An 'exciting new talent' who had been struggling for years. ❞

"Son, if you're going to do one thing with your life, finish that film," Vin, on CNN.com, recalled Irving advising him. "It was an important lesson for me to learn," Vin said, "to be thorough, to finish what you start."

Multi-Facial finally screened before a wildly enthusiastic audience of more than two hundred at Manhattan's Anthology Film Archives. Supporters rushed to offer congratulations. He sensed at once that his life had changed. *Multi-Facial* was invited to the 1995 Cannes Film Festival in France, where Vin was hailed as an exciting new talent. An "exciting new talent" who had been struggling for years.

Multi-Facial, which had been born of a need for artistic expression, now won acclaim as a pitch-perfect calling card for its creator. "I just went with it," Vin told the 1997 panel discussion attendees. "[I] said, 'Yeah, that's what I was trying to do!'"

Strays

After Cannes, Vin was determined to keep his momentum going. "I wanted to do something that I knew that I could make one way or another," he jokes, "even if I had to kill people for money." Fortunately it didn't come to that. However, he did something almost as drastic: He went back to Los Angeles and became a telemarketer. This time, however, he had a clear objective: Raise enough money to finance *Strays*, a full-length feature film he'd been writing off and on for two years. And he wasn't alone. John Sale, a former professional boxer, accompanied Vin to L.A. and worked the phones by his side. The two men, along with producer George Zakk, would become the core of One Race Productions, Vin's film production company. In less than a year, the trio scraped together $47,000, then flew back to New York and began work on *Strays* in February, 1996.

In *Strays*, Vin portrays a shady, oversexed street hustler who has had enough of meaningless one-night stands. When he meets a woman who opens his heart to a deeper relationship, he finds himself challenged by both his circle of eternally adolescent male friends and his own fear of the feelings he's hidden behind a tough exterior all his life.

The One Race team had enthusiasm to spare; what they needed more of was cash. They barely got the film in the can, and only after a rough cut won *Strays* an invitation to the 1997 Sundance Film Festival did they attract enough investment to finish it.

Strays' enthusiastic reception at Sundance paid off for Vin. He got an agent. He met producer Ted Fields, whose support would later help him land the lead in *Pitch Black*. Although *Strays* wasn't picked up for theatrical release, Vin was on a roll.

E! Online describes what happened next: "As the unofficial can't-miss kid of Sundance '97 . . . Diesel returned home to New York a changed man. . . . And then Steven Spielberg called."

"When you write independent film, not only do you think about all of your resources, but you've got to pick something that you know. . . . If you do a film that you know, you'll do it better than somebody with $60 million."

A happy Vin in NYC, 2002

Barry Pepper, Tom Hanks, Tom Sizemore, Ed Burns, Captain Dale Dye, Vin Diesel, Adam Goldberg, Giovanni Ribisi, and Jeremy Davies (front row left to right) in *Saving Private Ryan*

Chapter 5

Hovering in the Background

When you've got Steven Spielberg on the line, you don't need an astrologer mother to tell you that you're at a turning point. Private Adrian Caparzo's D-Day charge in *Saving Private Ryan* established Vin's film-world beachhead, but it was only, as Winston Churchill said, "the end of the beginning." Like Caparzo, Vin would have to beat the odds, claw his way forward, fight to capture and hold every inch of turf. He was still a grunt. But by serving with distinction he would rise swiftly through the ranks.

66 Try and stand out in a platoon of men all wearing the same uniforms and covered in dust and dirt. 99

Saving Private Ryan

Released:	July 24, 1998
Starring:	Vin Diesel, Tom Hanks, Ed Burns, Tom Sizemore, Adam Goldberg, Barry Pepper, Giovanni Ribisi, Matt Damon
Director:	Steven Spielberg
U.S. Box Office:	$216 million
Plot:	A squad of soldiers retrieves a comrade from behind enemy lines in World War II France.
What They Said:	"The supporting cast is uniformly excellent."

—James Berardinelli, ReelViews

Steven Spielberg had seen *Multi-Facial* and was so impressed that he invited Vin to the set of *Amistad*. Vin calls their meeting the beginning of his film career. The two men hit it off and Spielberg offered Vin a role in his next movie, *Saving Private Ryan*. The part hadn't been written yet, but Spielberg promised to create it. Vin said yes. After all, it was Steven Spielberg! Said Vin on Virgin.net, "I would have gone out there to shine his shoes!"

Vin was impressed by how open Spielberg was to the ideas of an incredible cast that included Tom Hanks and Matt Damon. "Here's a guy with more accolades than anyone I know, and more money than God," Vin marveled on Virgin.net. "And he's receptive?" The lessons learned while watching Spielberg were to stay with him. "After all the success, all he wants to do is make magic. If that's what he's going for, that must be the thing to go for."

Vin made the most of his small role, that of Private Adrian Caparzo. Discussing the part in *Time*, he said, "It was so small you might have missed me while blinking your eyes at the wrong moment. And try and stand out in a platoon of men all wearing the same uniforms and covered in dust and dirt." But Vin did. He managed to suffuse his small amount of dialogue with his unmistakable style, which is no easy job when one of your longest lines is, "Look, a Hitler Youth knife." But Vin made the part that was made for him uniquely his, which is certainly evidenced when another character calls him "smart-ass." Vin felt he had a terrific partner in Spielberg: "He's brilliant at making a gesture turn into a beautiful scene." An example, and perhaps the most "Vin" moment in the film, came when their platoon was under fire in a French village and they were being rained on. In the line of fire, Vin's Private Caparzo took the occasion to casually pick through a pile of rotten apples, gingerly taking a bite from one, tossing it away, then grabbing another as though he were relaxing at home. This nonchalance under fire and almost amused demeanor in a life-threatening situation is the first onscreen appearance of the Vin Diesel persona that becomes fully blown later in both *The Fast and the Furious* and *xXx.*

Not only did *Saving Private Ryan* have many firsts for Vin, it also probably featured a "last": Now that Vin is a franchise superstar, it is unlikely that we will ever again get the chance to see him in an extended bloody death scene like Caparzo's in *Saving Private Ryan.* But Vin has expressed very clearly what was most important to him about his performance and involvement in the movie: "In *Saving Private Ryan* I had one objective, and that was to bring honor to the soldiers that died."

Hard work had won Vin this opportunity; now he worked harder still. He underwent boot camp training along with the rest of the cast. When he wasn't on the set he was writing his next screenplay. Spielberg thought so highly of Vin's work that he allowed him to shoot footage for the second unit, a separate, smaller film crew that works in cooperation with the main one. The fact that some of these shots made it to the screen is an accomplishment that Vin boasts about to this day.

Vin's first major film role resulted in lasting friendships with many of the actors in the ensemble—Vin was to work again with both Pepper and Ribisi—

and their camaraderie certainly came across on film. They were all nominated for a prestigious Screen Actors Guild Award for Best Ensemble in a Film.

Vin also got to hang out with Tom Hanks and learn a little bit about how others have handled their stardom. Diesel told the *Star-Telegram* that when he was shooting the film he was wearing a pair of sweatpants that Hanks had admired. The Oscar winner asked Vin where he could get some. Diesel told him that the pants had cost $40, but he was sure that Hanks could get boxes of them for free. But, Vin recalled, "Tom said, 'No, I'd rather just pay the forty bucks, no strings attached.' I had no idea what he was talking about," Diesel says. "Now that I have a little fame of my own, I understand." Hanks also told Vin that the most important thing to learn how to do in Hollywood is to say no. The fact that Vin today has the confidence to turn down eight-figure paydays shows that he's learned this lesson, too.

After *Saving Private Ryan* wrapped, Vin relocated to a tiny West Hollywood apartment and continued to plan his rise to the top. He was more focused than ever. One day, *Saving Private Ryan* castmate Edward Burns visited Vin's apartment and found him making a list of every young actor who was more successful than he was, and exactly when he expected to surpass him.

"Vin has always been like that," Burns told *Entertainment Weekly*. "He's always had a very clear idea of where he was going and when he would get there. He's always talked as if he knew it was going to happen—it was just a matter of when."

66 After all the success, all he wants to do is make magic. . . . that must be the thing to go for. 99

—Vin, on Steven Spielberg

The Iron Giant

Released:	August 6, 1999
Starring (voices of):	Vin Diesel, Jennifer Aniston, Harry Connick, Jr.
Director:	Brad Bird
U.S. Box Office:	$23 million
Plot:	A boy befriends a giant robot that a government agent is determined to destroy.
What They Said:	"The most extraordinary—the coolest—Hollywood cartoon since the genre was revived ten years ago." — Rick Blackwelder, *Spliced Wire*

In *The Iron Giant,* Vin's voice was finally matched with a body of the same proportions, in this case a five-story-tall steel robot. Vin's acclaimed short film *Multi-Facial* was continuing to pay dividends. Director Brad Bird was gearing up for *The Iron Giant,* an animated adaptation of *The Iron Man,* a

Even when he plays a robot, Vin is hairless.

book written by the late English poet laureate Ted Hughes when he was focusing on children's literature, after the suicide of his wife, the famous poet Sylvia Plath. Bird, an animator since he was eleven, was still a teenager when animating icon Milt Kahl, one of the legendary "Nine Old Men" of Disney, took him under his wing. Bird went on to work on the acclaimed animated series *King of the Hill* and *The Simpsons*. *The Iron Giant* was a dream project for Bird, but he wasn't able to sell the studio on it until he pitched them the concept "What if a gun had a soul?" And with that angle, he sealed the deal.

But Bird still needed someone to play his title character, a gargantuan, misunderstood robot. Who had the voice of a giant with a kindhearted soul? Well, duh. An associate of Bird's who had worked with Vin at Sundance brought in a copy of *Multi-Facial*. Vin auditioned for and won the job over some of the biggest names in Hollywood.

The long hours in front of the microphone took their toll on Vin's voice. America's most famous rasp fell silent for hours after each day's recording session so that Vin's vocal chords could recover. Despite the punishment his instrument took during the making of *The Iron Giant*, Vin has no regrets about his involvement with the film, and has even expressed interest in doing a sequel. The film won critical acclaim and was hailed as one of the best films of the year and called "an instant classic." Though it did not do well commercially, it has since gained cult status, a path taken by another perennial favorite, *The Wizard of Oz*. It's ironic that the Iron Giant's line that most summed up his being and the theme of the movie was "I am not a gun." Vin delivered the line with all the poignancy required, perhaps sensing that in future roles a gun was exactly what he was going to become.

Reindeer—Used to Laugh and Call Vin Names

Vin Diesel still encountered some pitfalls on his way to the top, notably an ill-fated job on 1999's *Reindeer Games*. Miramax had lured Vin aboard the Ben Affleck action vehicle with the promise of a two-picture deal and additional development of his underdeveloped character. Shortly after Vin's arrival on the set, it became clear that all was not going as planned. *Rolling Stone* has reported Vin's version of what esteemed director John Frankenheimer, who died of a stroke this past July, said to him: "Frankly, Vin, I'm too old, too busy, and too fucking rich to worry about your character." Vin walked.

"I was inconsequential to the picture and thought I was leaving on good terms," Diesel explained to *Film*'s Bob Strauss. "Why should a director have an actor who doesn't want to do the role forced on him by the studio? It was unfair to Frankenheimer, and I was walking away from more money than I've ever seen."

But Vin was appalled to read, in *Premiere* magazine, a very different version of the events. According to Frankenheimer, Vin had been fired. The article made him seem like an egocentric villain. One rumor had it that he had refused to act with his shirt off (although close scrutiny of the Diesel oeuvre suggests that toplessness is not one of his hang-ups). From that point forward, some in Hollywood would label him "difficult."

"He has passion," said Universal's co-president of production Scott Stuber in *Premiere*, "and people who are passionate are sometimes misinterpreted as difficult."

Keith David, Rhiana Griffith, Radha Mitchell, and Vin Diesel (from left to right) in *Pitch Black*

Pitch Black

Released:	February 18, 2000
Starring:	Vin Diesel, Radha Mitchell, Cole Hauser, Keith David
Director:	David Twohy
U.S. Box Office:	$39 million
Plot:	Castaways fight for survival after their space ship crashes on a desert planet inhabited by hideous nocturnal predators.
What They Said:	"Vin Diesel's demeanor is refreshing and the combination of his voice and physical build make his character memorable. He's a one-man Eastwood, Schwarzenegger, and Snipes."

— Dwayne E. Leslie, *Box Office*

Vin's friend and producing partner George Zakk gave him the screenplay for a science fiction horror film entitled *Pitch Black*. Vin was immediately drawn to the character of Richard Riddick, a murderer whose surgically altered eyes offer a desperate band of castaways their only hope of survival. When the film begins, Riddick is a feared outcast, a loner who looks out for no one but himself. As circumstances thrust Riddick into a position of responsibility, he emerges as a leader and ultimately reconnects with his humanity. The character struck a chord. Vin has repeatedly named it the role with which he most closely identifies. "The Riddick character represents anybody who's been ruled out, given up on, prejudged," he told *CNN Interactive*. The same has been said of Vin Diesel.

Vin was determined to win the part. Backed by executive producer Ted Fields and director David Twohy, Vin auditioned again and again to overcome the objections of Universal Studios executives, who wanted a bankable star. Finally the executives conceded: Vin was the best they'd seen. Riddick was his.

Vin threw himself into preparations for the role. He imagined Riddick to be a man of stealth and grace, and so for the first time added yoga and Pilates to his boxing and weightlifting workout regimen. He also imagined a meditative aspect to Riddick, a Zen-like stillness in between his explosive bursts of violence, so Vin immersed himself in music and literature that would help develop the character's frame of mind. Clearly he was determined to make the most of this opportunity.

66 I'm flexing as much as I can to warm up my body! 99

Filming began at the remote Australian mining town of Coober Pedy, which was also the location for the Mel Gibson classic *Mad Max*, a film with which *Pitch Black* shared a cinematographer, David Eggby. Sunlight glittered gold on mineral-laced rock, creating a breathtaking landscape as wondrous as any computer-generated special effect added later. "A magical place," says Vin of the town, whose population of about two thousand people made it seem even more like the alien planet it was meant to portray. "I'm from New York," he laughs on the *Pitch Black* DVD, "I grew up in a building of two thousand people!"

All of Vin's preparation couldn't protect him from the perils of Coober Pedy. Although it looked like a heat-drenched desert on film, the location was actually freezing cold. Vin, as usual outfitted in clothes that showed his body off to its best advantage, suffered terribly in the icy wind. To make matters worse, the cast was regularly sprayed with water to make it look like they were sweating. "Torture," Vin calls it on the DVD. Fans may admire the muscles bulging through his torn clothing, but, in reality, Vin explained, "I'm flexing as much as I can to warm my body!"

There were other traumas. The effect that generated Riddick's surgically altered glow-in-the-dark eyes was a simple one: specially designed contact lenses. What could go wrong? Plenty. On the first day that Vin put the lenses in, they reportedly stuck tight to his corneas, prompting an urgent call to a specialist who had to be somehow whisked to the film's remote location to remove the lenses. Vin's eyes were rescued, but his damaged corneas remained a problem. Vin tried to avoid putting them back in, sometimes opting to act through Riddick's opaque black goggles instead. Robbed of an actor's most potent tools—his eyes—Vin must have been especially proud of the prep work that had taught him how to express his character physically. Even without his eyes, he could get the job done.

Vin's glowing eyes in *Pitch Black*

There's more. Early in the shoot, Vin did a scene in which he dove for cover while thousands of razor-toothed alien hatchlings (digital creations that were added later) swarmed over his head. Insisting that he perform as many of his own stunts as possible, Vin threw himself into the sand . . . and threw out his shoulder. The injury would trouble him for the duration of the shoot. Even tasks as seemingly harmless as wrenching open a door could result in searing pain. During one scene, Vin used all his strength to yank aside an old blanket, little suspecting that a crew member, worried about the wind, had unwittingly fastened one end down. The pain in his shoulder was enormous, though nothing, one suspects, compared with the pain of the crew member once he realized he'd almost disabled the star and risked a tongue lashing from the most frightening voice in Hollywood.

Not all of Vin's difficulties were physical. To more fully embody Riddick's loner status, Vin reportedly kept his distance from his fellow actors. This estrangement undoubtedly added flavor to the performances, but also caused stress within the cast.

After three trying weeks in the cold at Coober Pedy, the production shifted indoors to the Warner Roadshow Studios. (*The Matrix* was also shot there.) Vin might have assumed that things would go more smoothly there, but that was not the case. During a scene in which Riddick dislocates his shoulders to make an escape, Vin nearly did it for real. He came perilously

66 The real marvel of Pitch Black . . . is Diesel, whose voice seems to be emanating from some scary sci-fi sub-basement. 99

—Justine Elias, The *Village Voice*

close to losing an eye while tearing open his blindfold on a metal shard. When he was imprisoned for a long time inside the claustrophobic cryo-locker where Riddick begins the movie, he freaked out. "I literally lost it," he says on the DVD.

Despite all the trials and tribulations, Vin delivered a magnificent performance. He stands out amid a talented cast even in the first third of the film, during which Riddick spends most of his time locked up or on the run. Director David Twohy layers in close-ups of Vin even when he's away from the action, allowing his star to loom large. Though *Pitch Black* got mostly mixed reviews, Vin was singled out for praise. "The real marvel of *Pitch Black* . . . is Diesel, whose voice seems to be emanating from some scary sci-fi sub-basement," wrote Justine Elias in the *Village Voice.* "His Riddick . . . is the most sequel-worthy sci-fi creation since *The Terminator.*"

Those further adventures won't be long in coming. Work on the first of three sequels entitled *The Chronicles of Riddick* has already begun. Vin anticipates that *Pitch Black* will one day be seen as an introductory preamble to *Chronicles,* much as *The Hobbit* was for *The Lord of the Rings.*

So in the winter of 2000, Vin Diesel was on his way, launched by exactly the sort of film he'd enjoyed as a child. "I loved that Universal logo," he says on his DVD commentary. "You watch that logo as a kid growing up. Now I'm making Universal pictures . . . it's a great feeling."

Boiler Room

Released:	February 18, 2000
Starring:	Vin Diesel, Giovanni Ribisi, Nia Long, Nicky Katt
Director:	Ben Younger
U.S. Box Office:	$17 million
Plot:	A college dropout finds fast money and big trouble when he enters the high-pressure world of stock market telemarketing.
What They Said:	"Diesel is interesting. Something will come of him."
	— Roger Ebert, *The Chicago Sun-Times*

When Vin chose to join the ensemble cast of *Boiler Room*, he was making a strategic move; he didn't want to be pigeonholed as an action figure. He had more to offer than the brawn that met the eye and he needed an opportunity to showcase that. And he did a standout job. With his first line, in which he corrects a colleague with an erudite air, he establishes his character as someone who uses intellect, not muscle. Vin played Chris Varick, an experienced broker who takes a trainee, played by Vin's *Saving Private Ryan* cast mate Giovanni Ribisi, under his wing.

This time out Vin was playing someone of Italian descent who actually still lived with his mother! *Boiler Room* concerns a group of twenty-some-things working at an illegal Long Island brokerage house, a cross between *Wall Street* and *Glengarry Glen Ross*. In one of the more amusing scenes for Vin fans, Vin's character Chris gets up in front of a TV showing a famous scene from *Wall Street* and proceeds to say all of Michael Douglas's lines with him. Watching the scene in which Vin effortlessly closes a deal in front of a roomful of admiring colleagues, one pities the poor folks who took his telemarketing calls in real life. With that voice on the other end of the line, most of us would cough up our entire 401k plans. It's no wonder he raised an entire movie budget in just a few months.

With Giovanni Ribisi in *Boiler Room*

Vin, showing them how it's done, in *Boiler Room*

Not only did *Boiler Room* give Vin a chance to channel his real-life telemarketing experience into a first-rate performance, it also gave him something else he'd been looking for: the chance to make amends.

"I did *Boiler Room* to redeem myself," he told *CNN Interactive*. "To make *Strays* I telemarketed. I sold tools over the phone for more money than they were probably worth. Shameless job. You bother a lot of people by calling them. By doing this film, I put out the message that anytime anybody calls you to sell anything, hang up the phone."

Here's one for Vin trivia fans: At one point in the film a fellow broker played by Nicky Katt says to Vin, "Get your one-race paws off my money!" The "one race" line doesn't make much sense there since throughout the movie this character has only thrown Italian epithets at Vin. In real life One Race eventually became the name of Vin's production company. The "chicken or the egg" question of the day is, "Did he get the name from this line or had he been discussing it with Katt, who then chose to throw it in?"

Boiler Room firmly cemented the process that Vin began in *Saving Private Ryan*: He proved that he could hold his own against top actors with acting ability alone. He was now a commodity.

66 By doing this film, I put out the message that anytime anybody calls you to sell anything, hang up the phone. 99

With Paul Walker in *The Fast and the Furious*, 2001

The Fast and the Furious

Released:	June 22, 2001
Starring:	Vin Diesel, Paul Walker, Jordana Brewster, Michelle Rodriguez
Director:	Rob Cohen
U.S. Box Office:	$145 million
Plot:	A policeman infiltrates a gang of street racers that may be behind a string of truck hijackings.
What They Said:	"*The Fast and the Furious* may not have much of a brain, but it's definitely got a pulse. It's also got the sinister yet soulful Vin Diesel, my candidate for action hero of the new millennium."

—Andrew O'Hehir, *Salon*

The surprise hit *The Fast and the Furious* started out as an article by Kenneth Li that appeared in the May 1998 issue of *Vibe* magazine. Entitled "Racer X" (no relation to Speed Racer), it told the story of Rafael "Racer X" Estevez and the little-known world of illegal street racers in Queens. The article was brought to the attention of Universal Studios executive Scott Stuber, who saw the cinematic potential in Li's account.

Scott Stuber brought "Racer X" to a man who would play a significant role in Vin Diesel's rise to superstardom, director Rob Cohen. Stuber thought that Cohen, the director of such films as *Dragonheart* and *Dragon: The Bruce Lee Story*, might be ready to stretch his wings and take on a project that didn't include the word *dragon*. Cohen read "Racer X" and somehow resisted the urge to rename it *Draggin'*. He wasn't yet convinced that it would work as a film. A visit to a National Import Racing Association convention in San Bernardino, California, changed his mind. He remembered the moment for *Fade In*: "Here, the floodgates opened. Here were the cars, the racers . . . the clothes, the haircuts, the scantily clad Eurasian models like sirens pulling in the young males to examine everything from exhaust manifolds to computer fuel-mapping programs. . . . I saw the movie completely unfold—its texture and energy, its saturated colors and sleek designs, its freshness."

Cohen was particularly struck by the nonviolent mixing of black, white, Asian, and Latino groups, who referred to themselves as "teams" rather than "gangs." Regardless of race, respect was earned by whoever had the fastest car, the best sound system, the best-looking girlfriend. Any kid with a dream, determination, and a need for speed could learn how to transform an unassuming import into a high-speed "rice burner" and be a star. Cohen saw "a pure meritocracy," a shockingly harmonious subculture that had never before been depicted on film. It captured his imagination.

Cohen's interest in harnessing America's youth culture zeitgeist first made itself felt when he produced 1985's *The Legend of Billie Jean*, a film

Rob Cohen before (top) and after meeting Vin. Think someone has a little crush...?

about a brother-and-sister–led band of misunderstood, renegade anti-heroes (sound familiar?) who convert a sexy interloper to their cause. The film introduced Christian Slater to the world (just think, without Rob Cohen there'd be no *Kuffs*!), featured the two sexiest women of the early 1980s (Helen Slater in the title role and Pat Benatar on the soundtrack), and seems to be playing somewhere on cable television twenty-four hours a day.

Rob Cohen had heard the "difficult" rumors about Vin Diesel and the two men discussed it at their first meeting. Cohen wanted Vin to play the role of Dominic Toretto, a street racing king who is also the ringleader of a band of truck hijackers. It quickly became apparent that despite their surface differences (Cohen is a Harvard-educated film veteran in his fifties), the two were like-minded in many surprising ways. It was the beginning of a friendship as well as a collaboration. Cohen makes no secret of his regard for his star and praises him almost to excess at every opportunity. A typical Cohen assessment, reported by *MTV News*, reads, "He's got depth and truth and acting chops. He's got vulnerability, sweetness, and charm. And of course he's got ferocity and anger and can be very dangerous. For the women, of course, he's got a magnificent torso, a deep, gravelly voice, and a sense that he can protect them in all situations. In other words, he's the perfect action hero/anti-hero/leading man." Wow.

Since he and Vin first began working together, Cohen has shaved his head, pierced his ear, and rediscovered what he calls "the kid in me." Or perhaps he's gotten in touch with his inner Vin. He peppers his speech with youthful expressions and somehow gets away with it. Clearly the collaboration has reinvigorated Cohen personally as well as professionally. It seems to have given his libido a shot in the arm as well. Asked what he and Vin discuss during their frequent on-set huddles, Cohen gleefully answers: "Girls!"

Vin returns his director's affection, less breathlessly of course. He often cites confidence as the quality he most values—whether in a girlfriend or a collaborator—and Cohen's confidence is apparently a match for Vin's own. Few can make such a boast. While Vin may not spend much time giving flattering descriptions of Cohen's torso, he makes no secret of his high regard for the man. Vin has repeatedly said that Cohen's involvement helped persuade him to make *xXx*. And when pressed to pick a favorite moment during the making of that film, Vin selected not a frolic with a slinky Eastern European model, but a quiet moment alone with Cohen on an Alpine mountaintop during which the two comrades-in-arms reflected on how far they'd come.

His favorable impression of Rob Cohen was not the only thing that attracted Vin to the role of Dominic Toretto. Like *Pitch Black*'s Richard Riddick, Dom is both a leader and an antihero, a renegade on the wrong side of the law. Like Riddick, Dom's the best at what he does (in this case racing, not knifing people in the back), with a tough exterior that hides a riot of powerful feelings. Like Riddick, Dom is forced to reexamine the values by which he has lived when a supposed enemy makes a sacrifice on his behalf. The only difference is that Dominic speeds out of the movie exactly the same man he was when it began. Vin was intrigued by the prospect of playing a character without an "arc," in opposition to the unwritten Hollywood convention that demands its heroes change during the course of a film.

Among the passions shared by Vin and his director Cohen is the instinct to immerse themselves in the communities they portray. Unlike *Pitch Black*, *Redline* ("Racer X"'s new title) depicted a world close at hand. With the film's setting relocated from New York's outer boroughs to the Los Angeles hills, Vin was able to do firsthand research at illegal street racing events. "We spent most of our time running from the cops," relates Cohen in his DVD commentary.

The crowded street racing sequences depicted in the film that would ultimately be titled *The Fast and the Furious* were populated by real-life street racers, their supporters, and their cars. It's obvious from the way Vin interacts with the crowds of racers in their scenes together that he is completely at ease and has won their respect. Try to imagine any other contemporary Hollywood star inserting himself into the unruly, young, multi-ethnic world of illegal street racers, raising his arms like their king, soaking up their adulation, and looking for all the world like he belongs there. Some things you just can't fake.

Including real-life street racers in the shoot yielded unexpected dividends. Take after take of scenes that involved dozens of cars—sometimes engaged in high-speed evasion of police—went off without a hitch. Everyone involved was impressed by the skill of these young drivers, and by what they had under their hoods. Director Cohen has commented that if Detroit knew a fraction of what L.A.'s street racers know about cars, the U.S. auto industry wouldn't be in such dire straits.

The cast of *The Fast and the Furious*: Matt Schulze, Michelle Rodriguez, Vin Diesel, Paul Walker, Jordana Brewster, and Rick Yune (standing from left to right); Chad Lindberg and Johnny Strong (front row). Not quite *90210*

One would imagine that undertaking a film about street racing with a star that does as many of his own stunts as humanly possible would be a formula for disaster. Surprisingly, Vin was involved in very few mishaps. Some of the most hazardous-looking sequences, like the four-car street race early in the film, were actually generated inside a computer. Effects artists photographed the streetscape with a six-camera rig to create a seamless 270-degree panorama, then digitally inserted the cars. That's how the camera was able to swoop between and alongside the speeding vehicles. "There's just no way you could do a shot like that safely," said effects expert Bill Taylor in *Entertainment Weekly*. He also admitted to giving Vin's car a little more stability compared with his competitors'. "Because Diesel's character has this Zen experience at high speed, everything around him is smooth." No wonder Vin never broke a sweat—he never raced that race!

This doesn't mean he didn't spend a lot of time behind the wheel. To prepare for their roles, the entire cast took lessons at the Las Vegas Racing School. A lot of rubber burned before the cameras rolled. Co-star Michelle Rodriguez has fumed that while she and Jordana Brewster were restricted to 80 miles per hour, Vin and Paul Walker trained at higher speeds.

Second unit director Mic Rodgers came up with an innovation that enabled many of the film's hair-raising chases to be shot with an unprecedented degree of authenticity. He designed what was dubbed the Mic Rig, a truck with its sides, roof, and flooring removed that could accommodate an entire car frame in the back. Whenever a scene called for Vin to be behind the wheel, his car was loaded on to the rig and carted around at high speed. Vin could worry about his acting and leave the driving to others.

The only stunt mishap that involved Vin took place during the "Race Wars" fistfight. In the movie, a large security guard restrains Vin from dishing out any more punishment to his nemesis, Johnny Tran. Behind the scenes, the biggest punishment was dished out to the stuntman who played the security guard: Vin accidentally broke his nose with a backwards elbow!

Rob Cohen, in his DVD commentary, explains how an errant elbow could do so much damage: "Vin is a very, very strong person. Both as a character and as a physical entity."

Made for under $40 million, *The Fast and the Furious* brought in nearly $150 million upon its U.S. release in 2001. Although this was Vin Diesel's first real box office smash, he declined the invitation to do the sequel. It has been widely reported that Universal balked at his new $20 million–plus asking price and instead chose to go ahead with Paul Walker, who was available for much less. (Don't weep for Paul Walker, folks, we're still talking mid–seven figures here. Plus he's so damn cute.) Vin insists that it wasn't about the money. With sequels to both *xXx* and *Pitch Black* in the works, it seemed like a bad career move to lend his name to yet another franchise. According to one report, Vin's old *Pitch Black* castmate Cole Hauser will replace him in *The Fast and the Furious 2.* Jokes *Box Office Prophets*: "If you're getting a *Speed 2* vibe at this moment, you're not alone."

A race scene in *The Fast and the Furious*

A big gun with a big gun in *xXx*

Chapter 8

xXxtra-ordinary Success

If *The Fast and the Furious* put Vin on top of the world, *xXx* launched him into the stratosphere. But prior to filming, it wasn't clear that this was going to be Vin's star-making role.

Rob Cohen's recruitment of Vin to the film had an unexpectedly emotional component. Vin had been on the fence, leery of coming on board a project that had no finished script and an alarmingly tight schedule. Cohen made his pitch: "Xander Cage is a nihilist. Xander Cage is the least likely to save the world. Xander Cage doesn't care about the world. Xander Cage is recruited by the CIA to save the world, and in the process he learns patriotism and the value of life." The words resonated in late 2001.

"I grew up in a building where, if you looked out the window, you would see the World Trade Center," Vin told *Teen People*. "It's interesting that September 11 happened when it did in relation to *xXx*. There is some relevance. . . . Coming out of this experience, we all felt that frustration. We all, no matter where we are in our lives, wish we could do something, be proactive, make a difference—and Xander Cage ends up making a difference."

xXx

Released: August 9, 2002

Starring: Vin Diesel, Asia Argento, Samuel L. Jackson, Marton Csokas

Director: Rob Cohen

U.S. Box Office: $100+ million as of September 17, 2002

Plot: Xander Cage, extreme sports champion and world's unlikeliest secret agent, is recruited by U.S. intelligence for an undercover mission to stop a madman from causing global chaos.

What They Said: "The racially ambiguous Diesel cuts a fine action figure. He has the glacial swagger left over from his bouncer days and looks as if he's been bench-pressing Sylvester Stallone since he was twelve."—Wesley Morris, *The Boston Globe*

Xander Cage was introduced to an unsuspecting world as a James Bond for the new millennium. As continuously successful as the Bond franchise has been, the Bond character has been more or less frozen for forty years. Most teenage girls could more easily picture Pierce Brosnan telling them to be back from the prom by midnight, than accompanying them to the prom. Would Bond ever have worn the Gucci fur-collared coat Xander sported throughout *xXx*? As Vin put it, "To take nothing away from the Bond movies—I loved them—the Bond character is about as relevant to young audiences as someone like Clark Gable. I mean, Bond wears a suit. No kid today wears a suit." No cool kid, that is. In an interview with Roger Ebert, Vin said, "I think [Xander] is the voice of the younger generation. God help us." Ebert wrote that Vin then laughed at his own comment, but he may just have been laughing at Roger's suit. Either way, it's nice to know that the voice of the new generation is two octaves lower than the voice of the previous generation, and this time has an American accent.

With Asia Argento in xXx

Although a completely out-of-his-element 007-like spy is knocked off in *xXx*'s opening minutes, Vin and company mean no disrespect. They pay homage to the old-school spymaster's films with a metal-toothed villain that recalls Bond's nemesis Jaws (from *The Spy Who Loved Me* and *Moonraker*). Explaining the Bond films' influence in *Premiere*, Rob Cohen remembered *Dr. No* with a young boy's wide-eyed wonder: "I . . . got my first erection when Ursula Andress walked out of the water."

As Cohen told the Associated Press, "Just like you can't have *Dr. No* without Sean Connery, you can't have *xXx* without Vin. What Sean was to the '60s, Vin is to the 2000s." It sounds all very even-handed, but let's be serious:

Vin, one of the few men manly enough to pull off that Gucci coat

where Bond drinks martinis, Xander drinks Red Bulls. Perhaps James could take Xander in cocktail conversation, but it wouldn't be much of a fight.

Once again, Vin and Cohen included as much real-life flavor as possible in the film. Vin, whose extreme sports experience was minimal, undertook a three-month crash course in motocross, snowboarding, and speed climbing prior to filming. He also underwent Navy SEAL training. This led to some typical Cohen hyperbole: when extreme sports enthusiasts look at Vin, he declared, "they're looking at a mirror of themselves." If Vin needed some tips, he had an extreme sports dream team close at hand. The party scene extras included real-life extreme sports figures like skateboarder Tony Hawk, BMXers Rick Thorne and Mat Hoffman, and motocross stars Larry Linkogle and Jeremy "Twitch" Stenberg.

As usual, Vin did as many of his own stunts as possible. He reports being most nervous while shooting the scenes aboard the runaway Ahab watercraft, where a single misstep would have sent him tumbling into the frigid water. The producers worried about losing their $10 million man. Vin told *Entertainment Tonight*: "It was an issue on several occasions. Every time I went out on my motocross bike, our line producer, Arne Schmidt, would be out following me. But the only time I got hurt was on a snowboard jump in Austria. I got too much air, nose-dived and—whack!—landed on my back. Thank God the snow was soft."

Not every stunt mishap had such a happy ending. On April 4, 2002, veteran stuntman Harry O'Connor doubled for Vin during the scene where Xander Cage parasails behind the runaway Ahab on the Vltava River. It was a fairly simple shot, no big deal for an ex-Navy SEAL who had performed some of the toughest stunts in action films like *Charlie's Angels*, *Titanic*, and *The Perfect Storm*. Rob Cohen thought the sequence so routine that he delegated it to his second unit and went back to the States with Vin. The first take went off without a hitch. On the second take, however, something went terribly wrong.

Iva Knolova of the Prague police gives the following account: "He was being pulled at high speed on a paraglider and hit a pillar of the Palacky bridge. He died on the spot due to heavy injuries."

Describing his reaction to the tragedy, Vin said, "I took it hard. He was a special person. He was a wonderful, wonderful man." Speaking to *Access Hollywood*'s Tony Potts, Vin said, "I felt like I had wished I was still there. You think if you were there it could have made a difference."

Rob Cohen recognized the courage inherent in O'Connor's choice of career. In *Premiere*, the director said O'Connor's death "put a major dent in all our hearts."

E! Online's Anderson Jones reports that Vin, along with Revolution Studios (the company behind *xXx*), will establish trust funds for O'Connor's daughters, Hayley and Hanna.

A huge wreath of white flowers memorialized Harry O'Connor at the accident site. His Web site reads: "The world has lost a great friend, husband, father, brother, skydiver, pilot, stuntman, stargazer, celestial photographer, and so much more."

xXx's runaway box office success proves what everyone suspected after *The Fast and the Furious*: Vin Diesel is a Hollywood icon of the first rank. His attitude, however, remains balanced and realistic, the philosophy of a man who has not viewed success or fame as ends in themselves, but as necessary aspects, even by-products, of the work he wants to accomplish. When asked by *Cinecon* about when he will enjoy his success, he replied, "I don't know. Who knows? I'm just a regular guy. I come from a family of hard workers. We just think about the work and that's the most important thing."

❝ I think [Xander] is the voice of the younger generation. God help us. ❞

Knockaround Guys, 2002

Chapter 9

Coming to a Theater Near You...

During what only seems like a rapid rise to the top of his game, Vin made a few films that haven't yet made it to theaters. But his recent success will pretty much guarantee that you'll be seeing these movies soon.

Knockaround Guys

Release:	October 11, 2002
Starring:	Vin Diesel, Barry Pepper, Seth Green, John Malkovich, Dennis Hopper
Directors:	Brian Koppelman, David Levien
Plot:	Four sons of Brooklyn mobsters team up to recover a bag of money from a small Montana town ruled by a corrupt sheriff.

Filmed in 1999, just after Vin finished work on *Boiler Room, Knockaround Guys* found him reunited with yet another *Saving Private Ryan* alumnus, Barry Pepper. *Knockaround Guys,* a gangster movie with a reportedly comedic edge, cast Vin as one of four gangsters' sons who are dispatched to rural Montana in pursuit of that timeless plot device, the bag of money. Publicity photos show Vin slugging it out in a sleeveless shirt, a Star of David tattoo emblazoned on his mammoth biceps. But the chance to kick another butt or two is not what drew Vin to the role. He reportedly passed up more lucrative offers in order to work with a dream cast that includes John Malkovich and Dennis Hopper.

The movie wrapped in late 1999 and was widely viewed as a prestige project. Unfortunately, New Line Cinema has knocked around *Knockaround*'s release date six times. Vin fans are so desperate to see their hero in this film that there are several online sites with petitions to New Line demanding the picture's release. It's now scheduled to open wide in October 2002. We'll keep our fingers crossed. But just in case, here's some of Vin's dialogue to whet your appetites: "We find the toughest guy here, I mean the worst guy they got. The guy all the other guys cross the street to avoid, and we glaze this tough guy, give him the beating of his life. Way past the worst he's ever given."

El Diablo

Release:	Early 2003
Starring:	Vin Diesel, Larenz Tate, Timothy Olyphant, Jacqueline Obradors
Director:	F. Gary Gray
Plot:	A pair of DEA agents fight to bring down a mysterious drug lord.

The hearts of online gamers everywhere must have leapt when they saw Vin Diesel's name attached to a project called *Diablo*. Well, get your twitchy fingers off those mouse buttons, people; this film has nothing to do with the role-playing classic. In fact, in early 2001, Blizzard Entertainment, maker of the video game, filed suit in U.S. district court to keep New Line from capitalizing on the game's popularity. Shortly after Blizzard filed suit, New Line changed the title to *El Diablo*. The additional syllable didn't satisfy Blizzard and they eventually won an injunction that keeps New Line from coming anywhere near the word *diablo*. The film is currently known as Untitled Vin Diesel Project. Given Vin's current popularity, maybe New Line should just leave it at that.

Vin reportedly portrays Sean Vetter, a kick-butt DEA agent dedicated to stopping the flow of drugs into California across the Mexican border. When the arrest of the region's criminal kingpin creates a power vacuum, the ruthless Diablo, played by Timothy Olyphant, sees an opportunity to seize control. Diablo's evil schemes result in catastrophe for Vetter and his wife (Jacqueline Obradors). Hell-bent on revenge, Vetter and his partner (Larenz Tate) infiltrate Diablo's operation and employ brutal tactics to take it down. As things get more intense, the DEA agents question whether they have become as morally corrupt as their target.

Vin has an executive producer credit on the project and trained in the martial arts in preparation for the role. The film's release date has been repeatedly pushed back. Reports on its status are contradictory; one states that New Line has already planned a sequel, another that it's in desperate need of reshoots. The plot details that have leaked out suggest that Vin's role will offer him an opportunity to play unrestrained rage in a way we've never seen him attempt. With very few exceptions, the mighty icons he portrays are always holding something back, keeping their cool, refusing to lose control. The prospect of Vin Diesel really letting go on screen is chilling. It might be hard to watch, but we'll be there.

At the MTV Movie Awards, 2002

Chapter 10

Up Close and Personal

Though Vin guards his personal life as if it were the VIP room at Tunnel, there are some things we do know about Vin, the man.

The New York Times' A. O. Scott, in a review of *Boiler Room*, called Vin Diesel "the sexiest ugly man in the movies since Anthony Quinn." Vin has no problem with that. "It's probably accurate," he laughs. "I know I'm not pretty." Said *Playgirl* editor-in-chief Michelle Zipp in *USA Today*, "You can have too many pretty boys around. Sometimes you want a real man."

Leading Ladies

The rumor mill has recently linked Vin to many women, from Carmen Electra to Nicole Kidman (they were seen having lunch), but he dismisses every report about his personal life. For fun, he told *E! Online*, "My friends and I get on the Internet and find out who I'm dating." In an interview with the *Chicago Sun Times*, when asked if he has a girlfriend or whether women should send cards and letters, Vin said, "Send cards and letters. I'm looking. You just have to like big dogs who possibly wander into bed with you in the morning." The big dog is not Vin, it's his 175-pound mastiff, Roman.

Michelle Rodriguez

Stats: Born in Texas, of Puerto Rican-American descent, now a proud Jersey girl. Achieved critical acclaim with her demanding lead role in *Girlfight*.

The Connection: Vin and Michelle's steamy on-screen *Fast and the Furious* fling reportedly spilled over into an off-screen liaison.

Tidbits:

• Rodriguez on *The Fast and the Furious*: "It is about chick body parts and car parts, and working opposite Vin, who I get to make out with quite a bit, has really been great."

• Vin and Michelle were seen many times indulging in public displays of affection and the *Girlfight* star told Howard Stern on the air that Diesel "will be a part of my life for a very long time."

• It seems that Rodriguez is well suited to date another star. When explaining how hard it is, as an actor, to be in a relationship, she told the *Calgary Sun*, "Guys don't want to paddle along as if they're your lap dog." And we know Vin is more of a mastiff.

Best Quote: When asked by the *Calgary Sun* how she keeps her figure, she replied, "It really is all in the genes. If you want your kid to have a good physique, have sex with a Haitian."

Summer Altice

Stats: Born in 1979 and raised in California. Intelligent and athletic, Summer was named to the All-Academic Conference Team in 1998 while attending San Diego State University.

The Connection: Though they never shared screen time, Vin and Summer reportedly shared plenty of personal time in 2001.

Tidbits:

• She has a tattoo of a dolphin on the small of her back.

• She dated Limp Bizkit front-man Fred Durst.

• She was a *Playboy* Playmate.

• She was falsely implicated in the breakup of Helen Hunt and Hank Azaria.

Best Quote: "I got the nickname 'Spitfire' for a reason. I burned inside to play volleyball. I loved the competition of it."

Carmen Electra

Stats: Born Tara Leigh Patrick, this former Prince protégé found film fame when she trotted her lingerie through a lawn sprinkler in *Scary Movie*. Like Summer Altice, she once posed for *Playboy*. Hmm. . . . We see a pattern here.

The Connection: Gossips' tongues wagged when Vin and Carmen were spotted "canoodling" at L.A. hot spots in early 2001.

Tidbits:

- A precocious talent—at age nine she was admitted to the School for Creative and Performing Arts.

- Carmen had the unenviable jobs of replacing Jenny McCarthy on MTV's *Singled Out* and Pamela Anderson on *Baywatch*.

- Carmen's Vin connection came in between her relationships with basketball bad boy Dennis Rodman and former Red Hot Chili Peppers guitarist Dave Navarro. If he wanted it to last, Vin would've had to wear a lot more eye liner.

Best Quote: "I can actually have an orgasm from wearing tight jeans and driving a car."

Pavla Hrbkova

Stats: Czech model who was eighteen when she was hired to play a small role in *xXx*.

The Connection: Pavla's tiny appearance in *xXx* reportedly made a big impression on its star: According to *People*, Vin recently bought her a diamond and platinum ring!

Tidbits:

- Pavla supposedly spent the summer with Vin in L.A., until he had to leave to begin shooting his sequels to *Pitch Black*.

- *Rolling Stone* quoted *xXx* director Rob Cohen as saying that Vin and Pavla have "a beautiful relationship."

Best Quote: We don't know, she said it in Czech.

Asia Argento

Stats: Asia, officially named Aria, was born in Rome on September 20, 1975, the daughter of horror film director Dario Argento and Daria Nicolodi. She started her acting career when she was only nine years old. Since then she's been in over fifteen movies.

The Connection: Vin won a lot of praise for his performance in *xXx*, but the biggest raves came from this on-screen leading lady.

Tidbits:

- Asia's romantic relationship with Vin was on-screen only.

- Tattoos: two snakes and a sun—"It's over my ass"; an angel—"I did it there [rising from her pubis mound] not for some sexual iconography of a flying pussy, but more to hide it from my father"; the name Anna—"The last one I got, and maybe it's the only one I got for a reason. It's my sister's name." Asia's sister Anna died.

- Asia has a daughter.

Best Quotes: "I'm sure past boyfriends won't like it, but he's the best I've ever kissed" (talking about Vin). And in an article in *Salon* Asia claimed to have told Vin that she thinks he shaves his head to make it look bigger. Then she continued, "What he really wants is for something else to be bigger to impress the girls, but all he can do is shave his head."

Vins's Hobbies and Vices

Dungeons & Dragons: D&D has always been associated with muscle-less geeks and people who are more at home in Middle Earth than on the planet Earth. Well, they now have a new leader. Vin has played D&D for years. (He even buys the goofy little figurines!) In fact he named his stomach tattoo in *xXx* "Melkor" after his favorite Dungeons & Dragons character.

Yoga: Vin added Yoga to his workout regimen when he was preparing to play Riddick in *Pitch Black*, having decided that his character needed to be both graceful and centered.

Comic books: Vin was a big comic book fan growing up (which explains his initial interest in playing both Hellboy and Daredevil). Vin told IGN.com, "I had all the plastic-bagged comics and would spend the weekends reorganizing my collection." Between the superheroes and the D&D, Vin may single-handedly redeem an entire generation of geeks. If only he got the idea for the shaved head from Jean-Luc Picard. . . .

Snowboarding: Speaking to *The Black World Today* about his *xXx* extreme sports repertoire, Vin declared, "I already loved snowboarding," and spoke proudly of having performed some of his own jumps. One of these, of course, resulted in his most serious on-set injury.

Video Games: When Vin, as Xander Cage, urged his comrades-in-arms to "start thinking PlayStation!" he was speaking from the heart: Vin is an admitted video game junkie! For those who think it's just a phase, he had this to say to *Access Hollywood* on MSN: "You can be forty years old and playing PlayStation."

Cigarettes: According to the *New York Post* Vin smokes American Spirits— "a lot of them." "Smoking is the one thing I hate about myself," he told the reporter who caught him in the act.

"I miss my tank top."

66 I can no longer be just a guy sitting across from another cool guy just rapping about shit without every single word being loaded in some way. **99**

Life in the Spotlight

So how does a man with action figures on his shelves and a $20 million per movie price tag handle it all? Keep in mind that he's been expecting fame his entire life, but even for Vin the expectation and the reality can't always perfectly converge. So what does he do to keep it real? He remembers where he came from ("I celebrate the struggle," he told *Access Hollywood* on MSN. "I celebrate the climb"); he doesn't party too hard ("I haven't had a drink in two years"); he vacations in Europe with friends from New York, people who had his back long before he became "an action hero for the new millennium."

Last summer's trip, to Europe, was perhaps the last during which Vin could enjoy himself without being recognized, the calm before the storm of superstardom. Previously, one of the things he loved about his European summer escapes was the anonymity, the ability to walk around without knowing—or being known by—a soul. But on this last foray, each time Vin lingered too long in one location, the paparazzi trickled in. And this was before *xXx*. Next summer, the trickle will undoubtedly swell to a flood. Asked where he might ever again find anonymity, Vin suggested Romania. Perhaps we should look for him there next summer.

Yes, success has its downside, what Vin calls "the fine print you don't read when you're dreaming." Fellow passengers videotape him on airplanes. *The New York Post* lambastes his parents for staying in their federally subsidized apartment. Vin told *Premiere*, "I can no longer be just a guy sitting across from another cool guy just rapping about shit without every single word being loaded in some way."

Vin talked to *Gallery* about how fame has changed him: "I was an extrovert, the guy who was loud. The second I started getting unwarranted attention—attention without working for it—it changed me, and I started to become introverted. . . . I'm self-conscious about everything."

To cope better with what Vin has called the "bittersweet" nature of fame, he's talked to other stars who have had many more years of experience handling it, like Tom Hanks and Steven Spielberg. Unfortunately, according to Vin, "Their advice isn't that good. [Laughs.] I think I'm doomed. I don't think there's anything you can do."

Of course, when you're pulling down eight-figure paydays, there's always something you can do. For instance, Vin reportedly just installed a regulation-size basketball court at the Hollywood home he shares with his sister Samantha (she "looks like a female Vin," says Rob Cohen) and his mastiff, Roman (who looks like a canine Vin). Success has its upside, too.

Even being recognized by fans while on vacation has its advantages. Vin told *Gallery* about a trip to Cuba during which he unexpectedly found himself stranded without cash or credit and a big hotel bill to pay. Vin's quest for anonymity had succeeded all to well; they didn't know who he was . . . and they wouldn't let him leave! Finally a pair of shady characters—whom Vin suspected were in Cuba hiding from the law—came to the rescue. Why? They'd flipped for *Pitch Black* the night before!

A man and his dog: Vin and his Italian mastiff, Roman at L.A.'s Chateau Marmont

Chapter 11

What Lies Ahead?

When asked by *UniverCity* "Where would you like to see yourself in five years?" Vin spoke admiringly of Mel Gibson, and the hard-won industry clout that got *Braveheart* made. "I'd love to be able to make any kind of dream film I wanted to." That was two years ago. Vin's ahead of schedule.

So, what are those dream films? Now that this one-time doorman has the juice to open any door, what will he do with it?

Romantic Comedies?

ET asked Vin if there was anything he wanted to do that he hadn't done. Suprisingly enough, the action superstar said that he wanted to be in a romantic comedy! Vin loves the Clark Gable and Claudette Colbert classic *It Happened One Night*. He's claimed to have watched it hundreds of times and has been known to launch into perfect imitations of both Gable and Colbert from the film. Vin lamented to *ET*, "I don't see a lot of romantic-

Vin looking ahead in NYC, 2002

comedy scripts. It might have to do with the way I look. But I'll do one. Maybe I'll remake *It Happened One Night*. I've never waited for anyone to give me anything anyway. So, I'll just have to do it myself." Vin's already become the new Sean Connery, so Clark Gable isn't too dramatic a leap.

It's a Bird! It's a Plane! No, it's . . . Hellboy?

Though Vin has been a huge comic book fan since he was a kid, he has yet to attach himself to star in any major superhero film. It had been rumored

66 Hellboy is both a demon, a golem, and kind of an ape. 99

—Guillermo del Toro

Doing promotion for *xXx*

that he was offered the role of Daredevil, and passed. (Ben Affleck is Daredevil.) Vin also considered playing Hellboy, a Mike Mignola comic book character. The director and adapter, Guillermo del Toro (*Blade II*), seemed to want Vin for the part when he was interviewed last year. He also seemed to think Vin had the right look. He told *Ain't It Cool*, "And with Vin, how can I say it, well, with Hellboy he's a combination of him and [make-up wizard] Rick Baker. Because Hellboy is both a demon, a golem, and kind of an ape. He has the sloping shoulders, the long arms, and the brow and the mouth, almost a gorilla." Based on that description, it's easy to see why Vin didn't do it.

Knowing how Vin is, we imagine he's probably writing his own super-hero comic he can take to the big screen (or he'll end up taking Hollywood by storm as the next Superman).

But Wait . . . There's More!

Vin has agreed to reprise his role of Xander Cage in a *xXx* sequel. We'll be seeing more of Richard Riddick; maybe a lot more: *A Beautiful Mind* writer Akiva Goldsman is currently rewriting the first of three *Pitch Black* sequels that will collectively be known as *The Chronicles of Riddick*. And One Race Productions is developing an epic about Hannibal (the Carthaginian conqueror, not the cannibal).

Look for smaller, more personal films, too. Vin plans to approach Steven Spielberg about expanding *Multi-Facial* into a full-length feature. Vin's "sultry basso profundo" may soon be belting out show tunes: "I'd do a musical if I could," he told Virgin.net. "I'd do a re-make of *My Fair Lady* if they'd let me!" Perhaps there's an Oscar in store for the Hollywood star who most resembles one.

But not all of Vin's goals will be realized on the big screen. He confided in an MSN chat, "When I have a family with children, all my dreams will have come true."

In an interview with *Veronica* magazine, Vin quoted Al Pacino as saying, "A sudden breakthrough is the result of ten years of hard work." Then he added, "In my case twenty years." Vin Diesel may seem like an overnight success, but nothing could be further from the truth. His hard work, tenacity, and unshakable belief in himself make him as inspiring an icon as any he's depicted on the screen. Vin Diesel deserves all the success he has worked so hard for, a rise that had nothing to do with luck and everything to do with perseverance. If anyone is lucky, it's us, now that Vin towers over Hollywood and sees nothing but possibilities ahead of him. His memorable comment in *xXx*, delivered with a playful smile in anticipation of a long night with a beautiful woman, sums it all up best: "The things I'm going to do for my country."

> **66 'A sudden breakthrough is the result of ten years of hard work.' In my case twenty years. 99**

Vin doesn't need rose-colored glasses.